MY FIRST PUPPET PICTURE BOOK

Things That Go

Pictures by Tadasu Izawa

GROSSET & DUNLAP, NEW YORK

CARS
and
TRUCKS

It's moving day for someone. The men are carrying furniture and boxes out of the house and loading them into the van. When the moving van is filled, it will be driven to a new house. There the van will be unloaded. Then it will be ready for some other family's moving day.

Sometimes a whole house can be
moved on wheels. This house is being
moved away by a trailer—the biggest and
strongest trailer of all. A trailer such as
this one can also move large boats.

There are vacation trailers, too. Inside this one are places to sleep, wash, cook, and eat. What fun it is for the family at vacation time! They go on long trips, see many new places, and make new friends—without ever being far from their very own house on wheels.

In the morning a bus carries people to the places where they work—and brings them back home at night. Buses also take people to stores, or to faraway places. Many children travel to school on buses.

The police car with its flashing red
light on top moves quickly to the scene of
an accident. When there is a special
hurry, the siren goes WHEE-EE-EE! All
other cars make way for the police car.

The concrete mixer has a large tank filled with cement, sand, gravel, and water. The tank turns around and around. When everything is well mixed, the truck brings the concrete to where it is needed.

The dump truck carries sand, earth, stones, or even snow. The driver can dump the load, whatever it is, out of the back of the truck.

VROO-OO-OOM! VROO-OO-OOM! The racing cars make lots of noise as they race around the track. First one car, then another, moves in front. What excitement! The winning car and driver will get a big prize.

The gasoline truck is a large tank on wheels. The gasoline it holds is brought to the service station and pumped into big holding tanks underground. Now cars and trucks can stop for gas, then keep on going.

FIRE ENGINES

CLANG! CLANG! When the bell rings in the firehouse, the firefighters quickly put on their coats and boots and helmets.

FIRE DEPARTMENT

1

WHEE-E-E-E! The first fire engine
moves out of the firehouse with its siren
blaring. It is going to a fire.

15

The fire is in a building. The firefighters hop off their truck and attach a hose to a hydrant. The pumper engine will pump water high up and far out to reach the flames.

The fire chief drives up
in his special red car. He
tells the firefighters what
to do.

A fireman climbs up
a high ladder on one of
the trucks. He's going to
put out the flames by
spraying water through
an open window.

Now the fire is out.
The brave firefighters
get back on the trucks
and return to the
firehouse.

TRAINS

Woo-oo-oop! Woo-oop! The mighty diesel locomotive sounds its horn as it pulls into the freight yard. Many different kinds of freight cars will be hooked up to the locomotive for a trip across the country.

There's a boxcar. Do you suppose it is called a boxcar because it looks like a big steel box?

A boxcar has large sliding doors on each side so that workers can load it up with freight.

Next comes a flatcar. It is carrying some new tractors for farmers. Sometimes flatcars carry big truck trailers...or automobiles... or great big logs.

The hopper car is carrying gravel. A hopper car can also carry coal or sand. When it gets to where it is going, a worker will open a door at the bottom to dump its load.

A tank car has gasoline in it. A
refrigerator car carries fresh meat,
seafood, fruit, and vegetables. All of these
good things to eat must stay cold to stay
fresh.

Now—*bangety-bump!*—the tank car and
refrigerator car join the train.

There's a cattle car. The cattle in it have been rounded up by cowboys on a large ranch in the West. Now they are going to other parts of the country.

There's the caboose. This bright red car is the last car on the train. The conductor will stay inside, watching to make sure that the train moves safely and speedily, all the way to where it is going.

Now the freight train is on its way. It passes another train with people in it. Would you like to be one of the people riding on the passenger train?

AIRPLANES

An airport near a city is a busy place. Many airplanes can be seen. Some are coming down from the sky to land. Some are getting ready to take off and fly to faraway places.

People in the control tower are busy, too. They keep track of air traffic by watching their radar screens. They talk to the pilots by radio. They can see airplanes from far away, and so they arrange for them to fly in or out of the airport safely.

Here are passengers getting on a
jumbo jetliner. It doesn't seem possible
that one airplane could hold so many
people!

Inside the big airplane people eat, drink, and watch movies while flying high above the clouds.

These workers are loading mail and
packages on an airplane. Some of the
packages have special medicines which
must be rushed to sick people in
hospitals. The airplane gets everything
delivered very quickly.

Farmers use airplanes, too. This airplane flies low over the farmer's field. Sometimes it sprays plant food on the crops so that there will be more and better fruits and vegetables for people to eat.

Here is an airplane that floats and
moves along the water in a lake just
before it flies up into the air. It can also
land on the water. It is called a seaplane.

A helicopter can fly into canyons and along steep mountainsides. The large blades on top whirl around and around. A helicopter can even stay in one place in the air. When astronauts who fly into space "splash down" in the ocean, a helicopter picks them up.

Maybe someday you will see an air show. The airplanes twist and turn as they fly together in the air. Sometimes they fly upside down and do loop-the-loops, leaving smoke trails. Airplanes are exciting to watch.